If found, please call or email:

HELLO
my name is

email / phone:

This is my s.u.r.f. Journal Number [ ].

It records my s.u.r.f. sessions with God from __/__/____ to __/__/____ .

Also by Jack Nordgren

A Lake Surfer's Journey

Special thanks to:

My Dad for his example

My beautiful wife for her encouragement

Bruce Jepsen for the awesome photos

Wanni Wang for doing the layout

Allie & Abby Erkelens for proofreading

southshorefellowship.org

©2010 by Jack Nordgren. All Rights Reserved.

Photos by: Bruce Jepsen

Surfers front cover: Josh Nordgren, Nick Ingarfill & Alec Roberts

Surfer back cover: Josh Nordgren

Book design & Layout: Wanni Wang at BeFruitfulDesign.com

How To Have Daily Surf Sessions
With God

WHY READ THE BIBLE ?

My Dad read his Living Bible from cover to cover every year for 27 years. He not only read it, he lived it. A lot of people read and know about the Bible, but it makes no difference in their lives. My dad read the Bible and allowed it to change his life. The verse I remember him quoting more than any other was from Proverbs 4:11 in the Living Bible: "I would have you learn this one great fact, that a life of doing right is the wisest life there is." These words affected his relationships with his wife, children, and business associates. My Dad was different. Let me tell you his story:

His name was George Nordgren. They nicknamed him Buddy and that was soon shortened to Bud. He lived with his mother and father and went to church with them every Sunday. His dad was an accomplished musician and was the choir director in their church. He played the mandolin and sang with a group called the Swedish String Band at evangelistic meetings.

When he turned fourteen years old, things changed drastically. It was then he discovered that his father was having an affair with a young woman in the church choir. At that point his father walked out of his and his mother's life forever. Bud had to drop out of high school to help provide for himself and his mom. This happened during the Great Depression of the 1930's. Times were tough.

As he became a man he decided that he was going to follow God, no matter what. He decided to read through his Bible every year. That was when he began a more intimate relationship with God.

He opened a hardware store on Chicago's South Side with a partner. At first, they were closed on Sundays, but as time went on his partner insisted on being open on that day. That just didn't sit right with Bud, but he went along with it. He tried to explain it away by making excuses. One Sunday, while driving his eldest daughter to church, she asked him a question. "How come you're not going to church, Daddy?" she asked. He later said that he had an answer to that question for everyone else except her. He sold his half of the business and went to work at a paint company as a salesman. As a salesman, he could worship with his family on Sundays.

Some years went by and he was eventually able to buy back the business. He remained closed on Sunday. Slowly, the business began to grow.

Down the block from the hardware store, a meat market opened. Bud made friends with one of the owners. His name was Bill, and his business was flourishing. It was going so good that he bought a yacht. He invited Bud to join him for the weekend. "Come on! We'll have a great time! All these young broads (girls) are on the pill (birth control pills). No one will ever know," he said.

Bud didn't join Bill because he had a wife, a family, and a God who said, "I would have you learn this one great fact, that a life of doing right is the wisest life there is." Bill eventually lost his family and took his own life. He died a lonely, unloved man.

George Walter "Bud" Nordgren passed away on January 19, 2006. His family gathered to say farewell; his wife, his children, and grandchildren remembered him well and celebrated his life.

My Dad read his Living Bible from cover to cover every year for 27 years. He not only read it, he lived it. He left behind a family who loves him. He left an example to follow to our children and our children's children. He left a legacy. That is why I read my Bible!

Pastor Jack Nordgren

HOW TO USE
THE S.U.R.F. JOURNAL

Date: Write in the date, and don't forget the year. Someday you may go back and reread what you wrote about what God spoke to you through His Word. You'll thank me for having you do this!

Bible reading: Write in the daily reading. **The S.U.R.F. Journal Reading Schedule** goes through the entire Bible in one year. The daily readings include a reading from Psalms and Proverbs. My father used to say, "The Psalms help you learn how to get along with God, and Proverbs helps you get along with Man". You can choose readings for the day from the 3 different columns. You can do one, two or all three for the day.

Thanks: Write down 5 things that you are thankful for. Some days this will be easy and some days it will be hard. Don't skip this part. The Bible tells us in Psalms to enter into His presence with thanksgiving.

Title: Give your journal entry a title and write it down in the **Table of Contents**. Trust me—it will make it easier for you to refer to it later.

DAILY SURF SESSIONS S.U.R.F. JOURNALING When doing the daily reading, I want to encourage you to ask the Holy Spirit to speak to you before you start to read. The Holy Spirit can and will help you understand what the Lord is saying to you through His Word. The Bible says,

"But when he, the Spirit of truth, comes, he will guide you into all truth. He will not speak on his own; he will speak only what he hears, and he will tell you what is yet to come. He will bring glory to me by taking from what is mine and making it known to you. All that belongs to the Father is mine. That is why I said the Spirit will take from what is mine and make it known to you." **John 16:13-15 (NIV)**

S—Scripture—Ask the Holy Spirit to show you a particular verse or verses from the reading. Take some time to think about it. Write the Scripture reference and the verse down.

> "All scripture is God-breathed and is useful for teaching, rebuking, correcting and training in righteousness, so that the man of God may be thoroughly equipped for every good work." II Timothy 3:16-17 (NIV)

U—Understanding—Ask the Holy Spirit to show you what the scripture means. Look at the context—who was the writer speaking to, and why was he saying it? Is there a principle or example to follow? Is there a sin to avoid? What does this tell me about God the Father, Jesus or the Holy Spirit? Write down what you think it means.

> "As for you, the anointing, you received from him remains in you and you do not need anyone to teach you. But as his anointing teaches you about all things and as that anointing is real, not counterfeit-just as it has taught you, remain in him." I John 2:27 (NIV)

R—Relevance—ask the Holy Spirit, "How does this relate to me?" Once the Lord shows you the relevance of that particular scripture to you, there will be something you need to do about it. Write down how this Scripture relates to you.

> "Therefore, I urge you, brothers, in view of God's mercy, to offer your bodies as living sacrifices, holy and pleasing to God—this is your spiritual act of worship. Do not conform any longer to the pattern of this world, but be transformed by the renewing of you mind. Then you will be able to test and approve what God's will is—his good, pleasing and perfect will." Romans 12:1-2 (NIV)

F—Follow-up—what does God want me to do about it? It may be a prayer to the Lord or a plan of action for yourself. For example, maybe you would need to call someone to ask for forgiveness. Write down what your follow-up will be.

> "As the Father has loved me, so I have loved you. Now remain in my love. If you obey my commands, you will remain in my love, just as I have obeyed my Father's commands and remain in his love." John 15:9-10 (NIV)

As you are reading and journaling there may be some random thoughts or worries that come to your mind. When this happens, place them in God's hands. Write them on the bottom of the page next to **Psalm 55:22** and go back to reading and journaling.

> "Cast your cares on the LORD and He will sustain you; He will never let the righteous fall." **Psalm 55:22**

Letting God's Word change us is a key to Christian growth and maturity. There will be times that you don't feel like reading your Bible but that is the time you need to the most. Don't give up! It's like paddling to the outside through a big set—you need to just keep going!

> "Let us not become weary in doing good, for at the proper time we will reap a harvest if we do not give up." **Galatians 6:9 (NIV)**

Page	Date	Bible Reading

5 Thanks

Title

Psalm 55:22

TABLE OF CONTENTS

Date _____ Title _____ Page ____

Date _____ Title _____ Page ____

Date _____ Title _____ Page ____

Date _____ Title _____ Page ____

Date _____ Title _____ Page ____

Date _____ Title _____ Page ____

Date _____ Title _____ Page ____

Date _____ Title _____ Page ____

Date _____ Title _____ Page ____

Date _____ Title _____ Page ____

Date _____ Title _____ Page ____

Date _____ Title _____ Page ____

Date _____ Title _____ Page ____

Date _____ Title _____ Page ____

Date _____ Title _____ Page ____

Date _____ Title _____ Page ____

Date _____ Title _____ Page ____

Date _____ Title _____ Page ____

Date _____ Title _____ Page ____

Date _____ Title _____ Page ____

TABLE OF CONTENTS

Date _____ Title _____ Page _____

Date _____ Title _____ Page _____

Date _____ Title _____ Page _____

Date _____ Title _____ Page _____

Date _____ Title _____ Page _____

Date _____ Title _____ Page _____

Date _____ Title _____ Page _____

Date _____ Title _____ Page _____

Date _____ Title _____ Page _____

Date _____ Title _____ Page _____

Date _____ Title _____ Page _____

Date _____ Title _____ Page _____

Date _____ Title _____ Page _____

Date _____ Title _____ Page _____

Date _____ Title _____ Page _____

Date _____ Title _____ Page _____

Date _____ Title _____ Page _____

Date _____ Title _____ Page _____

Date _____ Title _____ Page _____

Date _____ Title _____ Page _____

Date _____ Title _____ Page _____

TABLE OF CONTENTS

Date _____ Title _____ Page ____

Date _____ Title _____ Page ____

Date _____ Title _____ Page ____

Date _____ Title _____ Page ____

Date _____ Title _____ Page ____

Date _____ Title _____ Page ____

Date _____ Title _____ Page ____

Date _____ Title _____ Page ____

Date _____ Title _____ Page ____

Date _____ Title _____ Page ____

Date _____ Title _____ Page ____

Date _____ Title _____ Page ____

Date _____ Title _____ Page ____

Date _____ Title _____ Page ____

Date _____ Title _____ Page ____

Date _____ Title _____ Page ____

Date _____ Title _____ Page ____

Date _____ Title _____ Page ____

Date _____ Title _____ Page ____

Date _____ Title _____ Page ____

Date _____ Title _____ Page ____

TABLE OF CONTENTS

Date _____ Title _____ Page ____

Date _____ Title _____ Page ____

Date _____ Title _____ Page ____

Date _____ Title _____ Page ____

Date _____ Title _____ Page ____

Date _____ Title _____ Page ____

Date _____ Title _____ Page ____

Date _____ Title _____ Page ____

Date _____ Title _____ Page ____

Date _____ Title _____ Page ____

Date _____ Title _____ Page ____

Date _____ Title _____ Page ____

Date _____ Title _____ Page ____

Date _____ Title _____ Page ____

Date _____ Title _____ Page ____

Date _____ Title _____ Page ____

Date _____ Title _____ Page ____

Date _____ Title _____ Page ____

Date _____ Title _____ Page ____

Date _____ Title _____ Page ____

PRAYERS

"I urge, then, first of all, that requests, prayers, intercession and thanksgiving be made for everyone—for kings and all those in authority, that we may live peaceful and quiet lives in all godliness and holiness. This is good, and pleases God our Savior, who wants all men to be saved and to come to a knowledge of the truth." I Timothy 2:1-4 (NIV)

Praying for everyone can be a daunting task. I would like to suggest a weekly schedule. Some may already have one, but for those of you who don't; consider this:

Sunday   Church Leaders Hebrews 13:18

Monday   Family Acts 16:31

Tuesday   Neighbors and Co-Workers Romans 10:1

Wednesday Missionaries Acts 1:8 & Ephesians 6:19

Thursday   Political Leaders I Timothy 2:2

Friday   Enemies Matthew 5:44

Saturday   Church Family Ephesians 6:18

JAN

Jan	OT Reading	NT Reading	Psalms	Prov
1	Gen 1-2	Matt 1	Ps 1	Pr 1
2	Gen 3-4	Matt 2	Ps 2	Pr 2
3	Gen 5-7	Matt 3	Ps 3	Pr 3
4	Gen 8-10	Matt 4	Ps 4	Pr 4
5	Gen 11-12	Matt 5:1-26	Ps 5	Pr 5
6	Gen 13-15	Matt 5:27-48	Ps 6	Pr 6
7	Gen 16-17	Matt 6:1-24	Ps 7	Pr 7
8	Gen 18-19	Matt 6:25-7:14	Ps 8	Pr 8
9	Gen 20-22	Matt 7:15-29	Ps 9:1-12	Pr 9
10	Gen 23-24	Matt 8:1-18	Ps 9:13-20	Pr 10
11	Gen 25-26	Matt 8:19-34	Ps 10:1-15	Pr 11
12	Gen 27	Matt 9:1-17	Ps 10:16-18	Pr 12
13	Gen 28-29	Matt 9:18-38	Ps 11	Pr 13
14	Gen 30	Matt 10:1-25	Ps 12	Pr 14
15	Gen 31-32	Matt 10:26-11:6	Ps 13	Pr 15
16	Gen 33-34	Matt 11:7-30	Ps 14	Pr 16
17	Gen 35-36	Matt 12:1-21	Ps 15	Pr 17
18	Gen 37-38	Matt 12:22-45	Ps 16	Pr 18
19	Gen 39-40	Matt 12:46-13:23	Ps 17	Pr 19
20	Gen 41-42	Matt 13:24-52	Ps 18:1-15	Pr 20
21	Gen 43	Matt 13:53-14:14	Ps 18:16-36	Pr 21
22	Gen 44-45	Matt 14:15-36	Ps 18:37-50	Pr 22
23	Gen 46-47	Matt 15:1-28	Ps 19	Pr 23
24	Gen 48-50	Matt 15:29-16:12	Ps 20	Pr 24
25	Ex 1	Matt 16:13-17:13	Ps 21	Pr 25
26	Ex 2-3	Matt 17:14-27	Ps 22:1-18	Pr 26
27	Ex 4-5	Matt 18:1-20	Ps 22:19-31	Pr 27
28	Ex 6-7	Matt 18:21-19:12	Ps 23	Pr 28
29	Ex 8-9	Matt 19:13-30	Ps 24	Pr 29
30	Ex 10-11	Matt 20:1-28	Ps 25:1-15	Pr 30
31	Ex 12-13	Matt 20:29-21:22	Ps 25:16-22	Pr 31

Feb	OT Reading	NT Reading	Psalms	Prov
1	Ex 14-15	Matt 21:23-46	Ps 26	Pr 1
2	Ex 16-17	Matt 22:1-33	Ps 27:1-6	Pr 2
3	Ex 18-19	Matt 22:34-23:12	Ps 27:7-14	Pr 3
4	Ex 20-21	Matt 23:13-39	Ps 28	Pr 4
5	Ex 22-23	Matt 24:1-28	Ps 29	Pr 5
6	Ex 24-25	Matt 24:29-51	Ps 30	Pr 6
7	Ex 26-27	Matt 25:1-30	Ps 31:1-8	Pr 7
8	Ex 28	Matt 25:31-46	Ps 31:9-18	Pr 8
9	Ex.29	Matt 26:1-46	Ps 31:19-24	Pr 9
10	Ex.30-31	Matt 26:47-68	Ps 32	Pr 10
11	Ex.32-33	Matt 26:69-27:14	Ps 33:1-11	Pr 11
12	Ex.34-35	Matt 27:15-32	Ps 33:12-22	Pr 12
13	Ex.36	Matt 27:33-66	Ps 34:1-10	Pr 13
14	Ex.37-38	Matt 28:1-20	Ps 34:11-22	Pr 14
15	Ex.39-40	Mark 1:1-28	Ps 35:1-16	Pr 15
16	Lev 1-3	Mark 1:29-2:12	Ps 35:17-28	Pr 16
17	Lev 4-5	Mark 2:13-3:6	Ps 36	Pr 17
18	Lev 6-7	Mark 3:7-30	Ps 37:1-11	Pr 18
19	Lev 8	Mark 3:31-4:25	Ps 37:12-29	Pr 19
20	Lev 9-10	Mark 4:26-5:20	Ps 37:30-40	Pr 20
21	Lev 11-12	Mark 5:21-43	Ps 38	Pr 21
22	Lev 13	Mark 6:1-29	Ps 39	Pr 22
23	Lev 14	Mark 6:30-56	Ps 40:1-10	Pr 23
24	Lev 15-16	Mark 7:1-23	Ps 40:11-17	Pr 24
25	Lev 17-18	Mark 7:24-8:10	Ps 41	Pr 25
26	Lev 19-20	Mark 8:11-9:1	Ps 42	Pr 26
27	Lev 21-22	Mark 9:2-29	Ps 43	Pr 27
28	Lev 23-24	Mark 9:30-10:12	Ps 44:1-8	Pr 28-31

MAR

Mar	OT Reading	NT Reading	Psalms	Prov
1	Lev 25	Mark 10:13-31	Ps 44:9-26	Pr 1
2	Lev 26-27	Mark 10:32-52	Ps 45	Pr 2
3	Num 1	Mark 11:1-26	Ps 46	Pr 3
4	Num 2-3	Mark 11:27-12:17	Ps 47	Pr 4
5	Num 4-5	Mark 12:18-37	Ps 48	Pr 5
6	Num 6-7	Mark 12:38-13:13	Ps 49	Pr 6
7	Num 8-9	Mark 13:14-37	Ps 50	Pr 7
8	Num 10-11	Mark 14:1-21	Ps 51	Pr 8
9	Num 12-14	Mark 14:22-52	Ps 52	Pr 9
10	Num 15	Mark 14:53-72	Ps 53	Pr 10
11	Num 16	Mark 15	Ps 54	Pr 11
12	Num 17-18	Mark 16	Ps 55	Pr 12
13	Num 19-20	Luke 1:1-25	Ps 56	Pr 13
14	Num 21	Luke 1:26-56	Ps 57	Pr 14
15	Num 22-23	Luke 1:57-80	Ps 58	Pr 15
16	Num 24-25	Luke 2:1-35	Ps 59	Pr 16
17	Num 26	Luke 2:36-52	Ps 60	Pr 17
18	Num 27-28	Luke 3:1-22	Ps 61	Pr 18
19	Num 29	Luke 3:23-38	Ps 62	Pr 19
20	Num 30-31	Luke 4:1-30	Ps 63	Pr 20
21	Num 32-33	Luke 4:31-5:11	Ps 64	Pr 21
22	Num 34-35	Luke 5:12-28	Ps 65	Pr 22
23	Num 36	Luke 5:29-6:11	Ps 66	Pr 23
24	Deut 1-2	Luke 6:12-38	Ps 67	Pr 24
25	Deut 3-4	Luke 6:39-7:10	Ps 68:1-18	Pr 25
26	Deut 5	Luke 7:11-35	Ps 68:19-35	Pr 26
27	Deut 6-7	Luke 7:36-8:3	Ps 69:1-18	Pr 27
28	Deut 8-9	Luke 8:4-21	Ps 69:19-36	Pr 28
29	Deut 10-11	Luke 8:22-39	Ps 70	Pr 29
30	Deut 12-15	Luke 8:40-9:6	Ps 71	Pr 30
31	Deut 16-17	Luke 9:7-27	Ps 72	Pr 31

Apr	OT Reading	NT Reading	Psalms	Prov
1	Deut 18-20	Luke 9:28-50	Ps 73	Pr 1
2	Deut 21-22	Luke 9:51-10:12	Ps 74	Pr 2
3	Deut 23-25	Luke 10:13-37	Ps 75	Pr 3
4	Deut 26-27	Luke 10:38-11:13	Ps 76	Pr 4
5	Deut 28	Luke 11:14-36	Ps 77	Pr 5
6	Deut 29-30	Luke 11:37-12:7	Ps 78:1-31	Pr 6
7	Deut 31	Luke 12:8-34	Ps 78:32-55	Pr 7
8	Deut 32	Luke 12:35-59	Ps 78:56-72	Pr 8
9	Deut 33-34	Luke 13:1-21	Ps 79	Pr 9
10	Josh 1-2	Luke 13:22-14:6	Ps 80	Pr 10
11	Josh 3-4	Luke 14:7-35	Ps 81	Pr 11
12	Josh 5-6	Luke 15	Ps 82	Pr 12
13	Josh 7-8	Luke 16:1-18	Ps 83	Pr 13
14	Josh 9-10	Luke 16:19-17:10	Ps 84	Pr 14
15	Josh 11-12	Luke 17:11-37	Ps 85	Pr 15
16	Josh 13-14	Luke 18:1-17	Ps 86	Pr 16
17	Josh 15	Luke 18:18-43	Ps 87	Pr 17
18	Josh 16-18	Luke 19:1-27	Ps 88	Pr 18
19	Josh 19-20	Luke 19:28-48	Ps 89:1-37	Pr 19
20	Josh 21-22	Luke 20:1-26	Ps 89:38-52	Pr 20
21	Josh 23	Luke 20:27-47	Ps 90	Pr 21
22	Josh 24	Luke 21:1-28	Ps 91	Pr 22
23	Judges 1	Luke 21:29-22:13	Ps 92	Pr 23
24	Judges 2-3	Luke 22:14-34	Ps 93	Pr 24
25	Judges 4-5	Luke 22:35-53	Ps 94	Pr 25
26	Judges 6	Luke 22:54-23:12	Ps 95	Pr 26
27	Judges 7	Luke 23:13-43	Ps 96	Pr 27
28	Judges 8-9	Luke 23:44-24:12	Ps 97	Pr 28
29	Judges 10	Luke 24:13-53	Ps 98	Pr 29
30	Judges 11-12	John 1:1-18	Ps 99	Pr 30-31

MAY

May	OT Reading	NT Reading	Psalms	Prov
1	Judges 13-14	John 1:19-51	Ps 100	Pr 1
2	Judges 15-16	John 2:1-25	Ps 101	Pr 2
3	Judges 17-18	John 3:1-21	Ps 102	Pr 3
4	Judges 19-20	John 3:22-4:3	Ps 103	Pr 4
5	Judges 21	John 4:4-42	Ps 104	Pr 5
6	Ruth	John 4:43-54	Ps 105:1-23	Pr 6
7	1 Sam 1-2	John 5:1-23	Ps 105:24-45	Pr 7
8	1 Sam 3-4	John 5:24-47	Ps 106:1-12	Pr 8
9	1 Sam 5-7	John 6:1-21	Ps 106:13-31	Pr 9
10	1 Sam 8-9	John 6:22-42	Ps 106:32-48	Pr 10
11	1 Sam 10-11	John 6:43-71	Ps 107	Pr 11
12	1 Sam 12-13	John 7:1-31	Ps 108	Pr 12
13	1 Sam 14	John 7:32-53	Ps 109	Pr 13
14	1 Sam 15-16	John 8:1-20	Ps 110	Pr 14
15	1 Sam 17	John 8:21-30	Ps 111	Pr 15
16	1 Sam 18-19	John 8:31-59	Ps 112	Pr 16
17	1 Sam 20-21	John 9	Ps 113	Pr 17
18	1 Sam 22-23	John 10:1-21	Ps 114	Pr 18
19	1 Sam 24-25	John 10:22-42	Ps 115	Pr 19
20	1 Sam 26-28	John 11:1-53	Ps 116	Pr 20
21	1 Sam 29-31	John 11:54-12:19	Ps 117	Pr 21
22	2 Sam 1	John 12:20-50	Ps 118	Pr 22
23	2 Sam 2-3	John 13:1-30	Ps 119:1-16	Pr 23
24	2 Sam 4-6	John 13:31-14:14	Ps 119:17-32	Pr 24
25	2 Sam 7-8	John 14:15-31	Ps 119:33-48	Pr 25
26	2 Sam 9-11	John 15	Ps 119:49-64	Pr 26
27	2 Sam 12	John 16	Ps 119:65-80	Pr 27
28	2 Sam 13	John 17	Ps 119:81-96	Pr 28
29	2 Sam 14-15	John 18:1-24	Ps 119:97-112	Pr 29
30	2 Sam 16	John 18:25-19:22	Ps 119:113-128	Pr 30
31	2 Sam 17	John 19:23-42	Ps 119:129-152	Pr 31

JUN

Jun	OT Reading	NT Reading	Psalms	Prov
1	2 Sam 18	John 20	Ps 119:153-176	Pr 1
2	2 Sam 19-20	John 21	Ps 120	Pr 2
3	2 Sam 21-22	Acts 1	Ps 121	Pr 3
4	2 Sam 23	Acts 2	Ps 122	Pr 4
5	2 Sam 24	Acts 3	Ps 123	Pr 5
6	1 Kings 1	Acts 4	Ps 124	Pr 6
7	1 Kings 2	Acts 5	Ps 125	Pr 7
8	1 Kings 3-4	Acts 6	Ps 126	Pr 8
9	1 Kings 5-6	Acts 7:1-29	Ps 127	Pr 9
10	1 Kings 7	Acts 7:30-53	Ps 128	Pr 10
11	1 Kings 8	Acts 7:54-8:13	Ps 129	Pr 11
12	1 Kings 9-10	Acts 8:14-40	Ps 130	Pr 12
13	1 Kings 11	Acts 9:1-25	Ps 131	Pr 13
14	1 Kings 12-13	Acts 9:26-43	Ps 132	Pr 14
15	1 Kings 14-15	Acts 10:1-23a	Ps 133	Pr 15
16	1 Kings 16-17	Acts 10:23b-48	Ps 134	Pr 16
17	1 Kings 18	Acts 11	Ps 135	Pr 17
18	1 Kings 19	Acts 12:1-23	Ps 136	Pr 18
19	1 Kings 20-21	Acts 12:24-13:12	Ps 137	Pr 19
20	1 Kings 22	Acts 13:13-41	Ps 138	Pr 20
21	2 Kings 1-2	Acts 13:42-14:7	Ps 139	Pr 21
22	2 Kings 3	Acts 14:8-28	Ps 140	Pr 22
23	2 Kings 4-5	Acts 15:1-35	Ps 141	Pr 23
24	2 Kings 6-7	Acts 15:36-16:15	Ps 142	Pr 24
25	2 Kings 8-9	Acts 16:16-40	Ps 143	Pr 25
26	2 Kings 10	Acts 17	Ps 144	Pr 26
27	2 Kings 11-12	Acts 18:1-22	Ps 145	Pr 27
28	2 Kings 13-14	Acts 18:23-19:12	Ps 146	Pr 28
29	2 Kings 15-16	Acts 19:13-41	Ps 147	Pr 29
30	2 Kings 17	Acts 20	Ps 148	Pr 30-31

Jul	OT Reading	NT Reading	Psalms	Prov
1	2 Kings 18-19	Acts 21:1-16	Ps 149	Pr 1
2	2 Kings 20-21	Acts 21:17-36	Ps 150	Pr 2
3	2 Kings 22-23	Acts 21:37-22:16	Ps 1	Pr 3
4	2 Kings 24-25	Acts 22:17-23:10	Ps 2	Pr 4
5	1 Chr 1	Acts 23:11-35	Ps 3	Pr 5
6	1 Chr 2-3	Acts 24	Ps 4	Pr 6
7	1 Chr 4-5	Acts 25	Ps 5	Pr 7
8	1 Chr 6	Acts 26	Ps 6	Pr 8
9	1 Chr 7-8	Acts 27:1-20	Ps 7	Pr 9
10	1 Chr 9-10	Acts 27:21-44	Ps 8	Pr 10
11	1 Chr 11-12	Acts 28	Ps 9:1-12	Pr 11
12	1 Chr 13-14	Rom 1:1-17	Ps 9:13-20	Pr 12
13	1 Chr 15-16	Rom 1:18-32	Ps 10:1-15	Pr 13
14	1 Chr 17-18	Rom 2:1-24	Ps 10:16-18	Pr 14
15	1 Chr 19-21	Rom 2:25-3:8	Ps 11	Pr 15
16	1 Chr 22-23	Rom 3:9-31	Ps 12	Pr 16
17	1 Chr 24-25	Rom 4:1-12	Ps 13	Pr 17
18	1 Chr 26-27	Rom 4:13-5:5	Ps 14	Pr 18
19	1 Chr 28-29	Rom 5:6-21	Ps 15	Pr 19
20	2 Chr 1-3	Rom 6	Ps 16	Pr 20
21	2 Chr 4-5	Rom 7:1-13	Ps 17	Pr 21
22	2 Chr 6-7	Rom 7:14-8:8	Ps 18:1-15	Pr 22
23	2 Chr 8-10	Rom 8:9-21	Ps 18:16-36	Pr 23
24	2 Chr 11-13	Rom 8:22-39	Ps 18:37-50	Pr 24
25	2 Chr 14-16	Rom 9:1-21	Ps 19	Pr 25
26	2 Chr 17-18	Rom 9:22-10:13	Ps 20	Pr 26
27	2 Chr 19-20	Rom 10:14-11:12	Ps 21	Pr 27
28	2 Chr 21-23	Rom 11:13-36	Ps 22:1-18	Pr 28
29	2 Chr 24-25	Rom 12	Ps 22:19-31	Pr 29
30	2 Chr 26-28	Rom 13	Ps 23	Pr 30
31	2 Chr 29	Rom 14	Ps 24	Pr 31

Aug	OT Reading	NT Reading	Psalms	Prov
1	2 Chr 30-31	Rom 15:1-22	Ps 25:1-15	Pr 1
2	2 Chr 32	Rom 15:23-16:7	Ps 25:16-22	Pr 2
3	2 Chr 33-34	Rom 16:8-27	Ps 26	Pr 3
4	2 Chr 35-36	1 Cor 1:1-17	Ps 27:1-6	Pr 4
5	Ezra 1-2	1 Cor 1:18-2:5	Ps 27:7-14	Pr 5
6	Ezra 3-4	1 Cor 2:6-3:4	Ps 28	Pr 6
7	Ezra 5-6	1 Cor 3:5-23	Ps 29	Pr 7
8	Ezra 7	1 Cor 4	Ps 30	Pr 8
9	Ezra 8-9	1 Cor 5	Ps 31:1-8	Pr 9
10	Ezra 10	1 Cor 6	Ps 31:9-18	Pr 10
11	Neh 1-2	1 Cor 7:1-24	Ps 31:19-24	Pr 11
12	Neh 3-4	1 Cor 7:25-40	Ps 32	Pr 12
13	Neh 5-7	1 Cor 8	Ps 33:1-11	Pr 13
14	Neh 8-9	1 Cor 9:1-18	Ps 33:12-22	Pr 14
15	Neh 10	1 Cor 9:19-10:13	Ps 34:1-10	Pr 15
16	Neh 11-12	1 Cor 10:14-11:2	Ps 34:11-22	Pr 16
17	Neh 13	1 Cor 11:3-16	Ps 35:1-16	Pr 17
18	Esther 1-3	1 Cor 11:17-34	Ps 35:17-28	Pr 18
19	Esther 4-7	1 Cor 12:1-26	Ps 36	Pr 19
20	Esther 8-10	1 Cor 12:27-13:13	Ps 37:1-11	Pr 20
21	Job 1-3	1 Cor 14:1-17	Ps 37:12-29	Pr 21
22	Job 4-7	1 Cor 14:18-40	Ps 37:30-40	Pr 22
23	Job 8-11	1 Cor 15:1-28	Ps 38	Pr 23
24	Job 12-15	1 Cor 15:29-58	Ps 39	Pr 24
25	Job 16-19	1 Cor 16	Ps 40:1-10	Pr 25
26	Job 20-22	2 Cor 1:1-11	Ps 40:11-17	Pr 26
27	Job 23-27	2 Cor 1:12-2:11	Ps 41	Pr 27
28	Job 28-30	2 Cor 2:12-17	Ps 42	Pr 28
29	Job 31-33	2 Cor 3	Ps 43	Pr 29
30	Job 34-36	2 Cor 4:1-12	Ps 44:1-8	Pr 30
31	Job 37-39	2 Cor 4:13-5:10	Ps 44:9-26	Pr 31

SEP

Sep	OT Reading	NT Reading	Psalms	Prov
1	Job 40-42	2 Cor 5:11-21	Ps 45	Pr 1
2	Eccl 1-3	2 Cor 6:1-13	Ps 46	Pr 2
3	Eccl 4-6	2 Cor 6:14-7:7	Ps 47	Pr 3
4	Eccl 7-9	2 Cor 7:8-16	Ps 48	Pr 4
5	Eccl 10-12	2 Cor 8:1-15	Ps 49	Pr 5
6	Songs of Sol 1-4	2 Cor 8:16-24	Ps 50	Pr 6
7	Songs of Sol 5-8	2 Cor 9	Ps 51	Pr 7
8	Isaiah 1-2	2 Cor 10	Ps 52	Pr 8
9	Isaiah 3-5	2 Cor 11:1-15	Ps 53	Pr 9
10	Isaiah 6-7	2 Cor 11:16-33	Ps 54	Pr 10
11	Isaiah 8-9	2 Cor 12:1-10	Ps 55	Pr 11
12	Isaiah 10-11	2 Cor 12:11-21	Ps 56	Pr 12
13	Isaiah 12-14	2 Cor 13	Ps 57	Pr 13
14	Isaiah 15-18	Gal 1	Ps 58	Pr 14
15	Isaiah 19-21	Gal 2:1-16	Ps 59	Pr 15
16	Isaiah 22-24	Gal 2:17-3:9	Ps 60	Pr 16
17	Isaiah 25-27	Gal 3:10-22	Ps 61	Pr 17
18	Isaiah 28-29	Gal 3:23-4:31	Ps 62	Pr 18
19	Isaiah 30-32	Gal 5:1-12	Ps 63	Pr 19
20	Isaiah 33-36	Gal 5:13-26	Ps 64	Pr 20
21	Isaiah 37-38	Gal 6	Ps 65	Pr 21
22	Isaiah 39-40	Eph 1	Ps 66	Pr 22
23	Isaiah 41-42	Eph 2	Ps 67	Pr 23
24	Isaiah 43-44	Eph 3	Ps 68:1-18	Pr 24
25	Isaiah 45-47	Eph 4:1-16	Ps 68:19-35	Pr 25
26	Isaiah 48-50	Eph 4:17-32	Ps 69:1-18	Pr 26
27	Isaiah 51-53	Eph 5	Ps 69:19-36	Pr 27
28	Isaiah 54-56	Eph 6	Ps 70	Pr 28
29	Isaiah 57-59	Phil 1:1-26	Ps 71	Pr 29
30	Isaiah 60-62	Phil 1:27-2:18	Ps 72	Pr 30-31

Oct	OT Reading	NT Reading	Psalms	Prov
1	Isaiah 63-65	Phil 2:19-3:4a	Ps 73	Pr 1
2	Isaiah 66	Phil 3:4b-21	Ps 74	Pr 2
3	Jer 1-2	Phil 4	Ps 75	Pr 3
4	Jer 3-4	Col 1:1-20	Ps 76	Pr 4
5	Jer 5-6	Col 1:21-2:7	Ps 77	Pr 5
6	Jer 7-8	Col 2:8-23	Ps 78:1-31	Pr 6
7	Jer 9	Col 3	Ps 78:32-72	Pr 7
8	Jer 10-11	Col 4	Ps 79	Pr 8
9	Jer 12-13	1 Thes 1	Ps 80	Pr 9
10	Jer 14-15	1 Thes 2	Ps 81	Pr 10
11	Jer 16-18	1 Thes 3-4	Ps 82	Pr 11
12	Jer 19-21	1 Thes 5	Ps 83	Pr 12
13	Jer 22-23	2 Thes 1	Ps 84	Pr 13
14	Jer 24-25	2 Thes 2	Ps 85	Pr 14
15	Jer 26-27	2 Thes 3	Ps 86	Pr 15
16	Jer 28-29	1 Tim 1	Ps 87	Pr 16
17	Jer 30-31	1 Tim 2	Ps 88	Pr 17
18	Jer 32	1 Tim 3	Ps 89:1-37	Pr 18
19	Jer 33-34	1 Tim 4	Ps 89:38-52	Pr 19
20	Jer 35-36	1 Tim 5	Ps 90	Pr 20
21	Jer 37-38	1 Tim 6	Ps 91	Pr 21
22	Jer 39-41	2 Tim 1	Ps 92	Pr 22
23	Jer 42-44	2 Tim 2	Ps 93	Pr 23
24	Jer 45-46	2 Tim 3	Ps 94	Pr 24
25	Jer 47-49	2 Tim 4	Ps 95	Pr 25
26	Jer 50	Titus 1	Ps 96	Pr 26
27	Jer 51	Titus 2	Ps 97	Pr 27
28	Jer 52	Titus 3	Ps 98	Pr 28
29	Lam 1-2	Philemon	Ps 99	Pr 29
30	Lam 3	Heb 1	Ps 100	Pr 30
31	Lam 4-5	Heb 2	Ps 101	Pr 31

NOV

Nov	OT Reading	NT Reading	Psalms	Prov
1	Ezek 1-3	Heb 3	Ps 102	Pr 1
2	Ezek 4-6	Heb 4	Ps 103	Pr 2
3	Ezek 7-9	Heb 5	Ps 104	Pr 3
4	Ezek 10-11	Heb 6	Ps 105:1-23	Pr 4
5	Ezek 12-13	Heb 7:1-17	Ps 105:24-45	Pr 5
6	Ezek 14-16	Heb 7:18-28	Ps 106:1-12	Pr 6
7	Ezek 17	Heb 8	Ps 106:13-31	Pr 7
8	Ezek 18-19	Heb 9:1-10	Ps 106:32-48	Pr 8
9	Ezek 20	Heb 9:11-28	Ps 107	Pr 9
10	Ezek 21-22	Heb 10:1-17	Ps 108	Pr 10
11	Ezek 23	Heb 10:18-39	Ps 109	Pr 11
12	Ezek 24-26	Heb 11:1-16	Ps 110	Pr 12
13	Ezek 27-28	Heb 11:17-31	Ps 111	Pr 13
14	Ezek 29-30	Heb 11:32-12:13	Ps 112	Pr 14
15	Ezek 31-32	Heb 12:14-29	Ps 113	Pr 15
16	Ezek 33-34	Heb 13	Ps 114	Pr 16
17	Ezek 35-36	James 1:1-18	Ps 115	Pr 17
18	Ezek 37-38	James 1:19-2:17	Ps 116	Pr 18
19	Ezek 39-40	James 2:18-3:18	Ps 117	Pr 19
20	Ezek 41	James 4	Ps 118	Pr 20
21	Ezek 42-43	James 5	Ps 119:1-16	Pr 21
22	Ezek 44	1 Pet 1	Ps 119:17-32	Pr 22
23	Ezek 45-46	1 Pet 2	Ps 119:33-48	Pr 23
24	Ezek 47-48	1 Pet 3	Ps 119:49-64	Pr 24
25	Dan 1-2	1 Pet 4	Ps 119:65-80	Pr 25
26	Dan 3	1 Pet 5	Ps 119:81-96	Pr 26
27	Dan 4	2 Pet 1	Ps 119:97-112	Pr 27
28	Dan 5	2 Pet 2	Ps 119:113-128	Pr 28
29	Dan 6	2 Pet 3	Ps 119:129-152	Pr 29
30	Dan 7	1 John 1	Ps 119:153-176	Pr 30-31

Dec	OT Reading	NT Reading	Psalms	Prov
1	Dan 8	1 John 2	Ps 120	Pr 1
2	Dan 9-10	1 John 3	Ps 121	Pr 2
3	Dan 11	1 John 4	Ps 122	Pr 3
4	Dan 12	1 John 5:1-10	Ps 123	Pr 4
5	Hosea 1-3	1 John 5:11-21	Ps 124	Pr 5
6	Hosea 4-5	2 John	Ps 125	Pr 6
7	Hosea 6-9	3 John	Ps 126	Pr 7
8	Hosea 10-14	Jude	Ps 127	Pr 8
9	Joel	Rev 1	Ps 128	Pr 9
10	Amos 1-3	Rev 2:1-17	Ps 129	Pr 10
11	Amos 4-6	Rev 2:18-3:6	Ps 130	Pr 11
12	Amos 7-9	Rev 3:7-22	Ps 131	Pr 12
13	Obad	Rev 4	Ps 132	Pr 13
14	Jonah	Rev 5	Ps 133	Pr 14
15	Micah 1-4	Rev 6	Ps 134	Pr 15
16	Micah 5-7	Rev 7	Ps 135	Pr 16
17	Nahum	Rev 8	Ps 136	Pr 17
18	Habbakuk	Rev 9	Ps 137	Pr 18
19	Zephaniah	Rev 10	Ps 138	Pr 19
20	Haggai	Rev 11	Ps 139	Pr 20
21	Zech 1	Rev 12	Ps 140	Pr 21
22	Zech 2-3	Rev 13	Ps 141	Pr 22
23	Zech 4-5	Rev 14	Ps 142	Pr 23
24	Zech 6-7	Rev 15	Ps 143	Pr 24
25	Zech 8	Rev 16	Ps 144	Pr 25
26	Zech 9	Rev 17	Ps 145	Pr 26
27	Zech 10-11	Rev 18	Ps 146	Pr 27
28	Zech 12-13	Rev 19	Ps 147	Pr 28
29	Zech 14	Rev 20	Ps 148	Pr 29
30	Mal 1-2	Rev 21	Ps 149	Pr 30
31	Mal 3-4	Rev 22	Ps 150	Pr 31

Page	Date	Bible Reading

5 Thanks

Title

_____

_____

_____

_____

_____

_____

_____

_____

_____

_____

_____

_____

_____

_____

Psalm 55:22

Bible Reading

Date

Page

5 Thanks

Title

_____

_____

_____

_____

_____

_____

_____

_____

_____

_____

_____

_____

_____

_____

_____

_____

_____

_____

Psalm 55:22

Page	Date	Bible Reading

5 Thanks

Title

Psalm 55:22

Bible Reading	Date	Page

5 Thanks

Title

_____

_____

_____

_____

_____

_____

_____

_____

_____

_____

_____

_____

_____

_____

_____

_____

_____

Psalm 55:22

Page	Date	Bible Reading

5 Thanks

Title

Psalm 55:22

Bible Reading	Date	Page

5 Thanks

Title

_____

_____

_____

_____

_____

_____

_____

_____

_____

_____

_____

_____

_____

_____

_____

_____

_____

Psalm 55:22

Page	Date	Bible Reading

5 Thanks

Title

_____

_____

_____

_____

_____

_____

_____

_____

_____

_____

_____

_____

_____

_____

Psalm 55:22

Bible Reading	Date	Page

5 Thanks

Title

_____

_____

_____

_____

_____

_____

_____

_____

_____

_____

_____

_____

_____

_____

_____

_____

_____

_____

_____

Psalm 55:22

Page	Date	Bible Reading

5 Thanks

Title

_____

_____

_____

_____

_____

_____

_____

_____

_____

_____

_____

_____

_____

_____

Psalm 55:22

Bible Reading	Date	Page

5 Thanks

Title

_____

_____

_____

_____

_____

_____

_____

_____

_____

_____

_____

_____

_____

_____

_____

_____

_____

Psalm 55:22

Page	Date	Bible Reading

5 Thanks

Title

Psalm 55:22

Bible Reading	Date	Page

5 Thanks

Title

Psalm 55:22

Page	Date	Bible Reading

5 Thanks

Title

_____

_____

_____

_____

_____

_____

_____

_____

_____

_____

_____

_____

_____

_____

Psalm 55:22

Bible Reading	Date	Page

5 Thanks

Title

_____

_____

_____

_____

_____

_____

_____

_____

_____

_____

_____

_____

_____

_____

_____

_____

_____

_____

_____

Psalm 55:22

Page	Date	Bible Reading

5 Thanks

Title

_____

_____

_____

_____

_____

_____

_____

_____

_____

_____

_____

_____

_____

_____

_____

_____

Psalm 55:22

Bible Reading

Date

Page

5 Thanks

Title

Psalm 55:22

Page	Date	Bible Reading

5 Thanks

Title

Psalm 55:22

Bible Reading	Date	Page

5 Thanks

Title

_____

_____

_____

_____

_____

_____

_____

_____

_____

_____

_____

_____

_____

_____

_____

_____

_____

_____

Psalm 55:22

Page	Date	Bible Reading

5 Thanks

Title

Psalm 55:22

Bible Reading	Date	Page

5 Thanks

Title

Psalm 55:22

Page	Date	Bible Reading

5 Thanks

Title

_____

_____

_____

_____

_____

_____

_____

_____

_____

_____

_____

_____

_____

_____

Psalm 55:22

Bible Reading	Date	Page

5 Thanks

Title

Psalm 55:22

Page	Date	Bible Reading

5 Thanks

Title

Psalm 55:22

Bible Reading	Date	Page

5 Thanks

Title

_____

_____

_____

_____

_____

_____

_____

_____

_____

_____

_____

_____

_____

_____

_____

_____

_____

_____

Psalm 55:22

Page	Date	Bible Reading

5 Thanks

Title

_____

_____

_____

_____

_____

_____

_____

_____

_____

_____

_____

_____

_____

Psalm 55:22

Bible Reading **Date** **Page**

5 Thanks

Title

_____

_____

_____

_____

_____

_____

_____

_____

_____

_____

_____

_____

_____

_____

_____

_____

_____

Psalm 55:22

Page	Date	Bible Reading

5 Thanks

Title

Psalm 55:22

Bible Reading	Date	Page

5 Thanks

Title

Psalm 55:22

Page	Date	Bible Reading

5 Thanks

Title

Psalm 55:22

Bible Reading	Date	Page

5 Thanks

Title

_____

_____

_____

_____

_____

_____

_____

_____

_____

_____

_____

_____

_____

_____

_____

_____

_____

_____

_____

Psalm 55:22

Page	Date	Bible Reading

5 Thanks

Title

_____

_____

_____

_____

_____

_____

_____

_____

_____

_____

_____

_____

_____

_____

_____

Psalm 55:22

Bible Reading	Date	Page

5 Thanks

Title

_____

_____

_____

_____

_____

_____

_____

_____

_____

_____

_____

_____

_____

_____

_____

_____

_____

_____

_____

Psalm 55:22

Page	Date	Bible Reading

5 Thanks

Title

Psalm 55:22

Bible Reading	Date	Page

5 Thanks

Title

Psalm 55:22

Page	Date	Bible Reading

5 Thanks

Title

Psalm 55:22

Bible Reading	Date	Page

5 Thanks

Title

Psalm 55:22

Page	Date	Bible Reading

5 Thanks

Title

_____

_____

_____

_____

_____

_____

_____

_____

_____

_____

_____

_____

_____

_____

Psalm 55:22

Bible Reading

Date

Page

5 Thanks

Title

_____

_____

_____

_____

_____

_____

_____

_____

_____

_____

_____

_____

_____

_____

_____

_____

_____

_____

_____

Psalm 55:22

Page	Date	Bible Reading

5 Thanks

Title

_____

_____

_____

_____

_____

_____

_____

_____

_____

_____

_____

_____

_____

_____

_____

_____

Psalm 55:22

Bible Reading

Date

Page

5 Thanks

Title

Psalm 55:22

Page	Date	Bible Reading

5 Thanks

Title

Psalm 55:22

Bible Reading	Date	Page

5 Thanks

Title

_____

_____

_____

_____

_____

_____

_____

_____

_____

_____

_____

_____

_____

_____

_____

_____

_____

_____

Psalm 55:22

Page	Date	Bible Reading

5 Thanks

Title

Psalm 55:22

Bible Reading

Date

Page

5 Thanks

Title

Psalm 55:22

Page	Date	Bible Reading

5 Thanks

Title

Psalm 55:22

Bible Reading	Date	Page

5 Thanks

Title

Psalm 55:22

Page	Date	Bible Reading

5 Thanks

Title

Psalm 55:22

Bible Reading	Date	Page

5 Thanks

Title

Psalm 55:22

Page	Date	Bible Reading

5 Thanks

Title

Psalm 55:22

Bible Reading	Date	Page

5 Thanks

Title

_____

_____

_____

_____

_____

_____

_____

_____

_____

_____

_____

_____

_____

_____

_____

_____

Psalm 55:22

Page	Date	Bible Reading

5 Thanks

Title

Psalm 55:22

Bible Reading	Date	Page

5 Thanks

Title

Psalm 55:22

Page	Date	Bible Reading

5 Thanks

Title

_____

_____

_____

_____

_____

_____

_____

_____

_____

_____

_____

_____

_____

_____

_____

_____

Psalm 55:22

Bible Reading		Date	Page

5 Thanks

Title

_____

_____

_____

_____

_____

_____

_____

_____

_____

_____

_____

_____

_____

_____

_____

_____

_____

_____

Psalm 55:22

Page	Date	Bible Reading

5 Thanks

Title

Psalm 55:22

Bible Reading	Date	Page

5 Thanks

Title

Psalm 55:22

Page	Date	Bible Reading

5 Thanks

Title

Psalm 55:22

Bible Reading	Date	Page

5 Thanks

Title

Psalm 55:22

Page	Date	Bible Reading

5 Thanks

Title

Psalm 55:22

Bible Reading

Date

Page

5 Thanks

Title

Psalm 55:22

Page	Date	Bible Reading

5 Thanks

Title

Psalm 55:22

Bible Reading

Date

Page

5 Thanks

Title

Psalm 55:22

Page	Date	Bible Reading

5 Thanks

Title

Psalm 55:22

Bible Reading

Date

Page

5 Thanks

Title

Psalm 55:22

Page	Date	Bible Reading

5 Thanks

Title

Psalm 55:22

Bible Reading	Date	Page

5 Thanks

Title

Psalm 55:22

Page	Date	Bible Reading

5 Thanks

Title

Psalm 55:22

Bible Reading	Date	Page

5 Thanks

Title

Psalm 55:22

Page	Date	Bible Reading

5 Thanks

Title

_____

_____

_____

_____

_____

_____

_____

_____

_____

_____

_____

_____

_____

_____

_____

_____

_____

Psalm 55:22

Bible Reading	Date	Page

5 Thanks

Title

Psalm 55:22

Page	Date	Bible Reading

5 Thanks

Title

_____

_____

_____

_____

_____

_____

_____

_____

_____

_____

_____

_____

_____

_____

_____

_____

Psalm 55:22

Bible Reading

Date

Page

5 Thanks

Title

Psalm 55:22

Page	Date	Bible Reading

5 Thanks

Title

Psalm 55:22

Bible Reading	Date	Page

5 Thanks

Title

_____

_____

_____

_____

_____

_____

_____

_____

_____

_____

_____

_____

_____

_____

_____

_____

Psalm 55:22

Page	Date	Bible Reading

5 Thanks

Title

_____

_____

_____

_____

_____

_____

_____

_____

_____

_____

_____

_____

_____

_____

Psalm 55:22

Bible Reading

Date

Page

5 Thanks

Title

_____

_____

_____

_____

_____

_____

_____

_____

_____

_____

_____

_____

_____

_____

_____

_____

Psalm 55:22

Page	Date	Bible Reading

5 Thanks

Title

Psalm 55:22

Bible Reading	Date	Page

5 Thanks

Title

Psalm 55:22

Page	Date	Bible Reading

5 Thanks

Title

Psalm 55:22

Bible Reading	Date	Page

5 Thanks

Title

_____

_____

_____

_____

_____

_____

_____

_____

_____

_____

_____

_____

_____

_____

_____

_____

_____

Psalm 55:22

Page	Date	Bible Reading

5 Thanks

Title

_____

_____

_____

_____

_____

_____

_____

_____

_____

_____

_____

_____

_____

_____

_____

_____

_____

Psalm 55:22

Bible Reading	Date	Page

5 Thanks

Title

Psalm 55:22

Page	Date	Bible Reading

5 Thanks

Title

Psalm 55:22

Bible Reading	Date	Page

5 Thanks

Title

Psalm 55:22

Page	Date	Bible Reading

5 Thanks

Title

Psalm 55:22

Bible Reading	Date	Page

5 Thanks

Title

_____

_____

_____

_____

_____

_____

_____

_____

_____

_____

_____

_____

_____

_____

_____

_____

Psalm 55:22

Page	Date	Bible Reading

5 Thanks

Title

_____

_____

_____

_____

_____

_____

_____

_____

_____

_____

_____

_____

_____

_____

Psalm 55:22

Bible Reading	Date	Page

5 Thanks

Title

_____

_____

_____

_____

_____

_____

_____

_____

_____

_____

_____

_____

_____

_____

_____

_____

Psalm 55:22

Page	Date	Bible Reading

5 Thanks

Title

Psalm 55:22

Bible Reading

Date

Page

5 Thanks

Title

_____

_____

_____

_____

_____

_____

_____

_____

_____

_____

_____

_____

_____

_____

_____

_____

_____

Psalm 55:22

Page	Date	Bible Reading

5 Thanks

Title

_____

_____

_____

_____

_____

_____

_____

_____

_____

_____

_____

_____

_____

_____

_____

Psalm 55:22

Bible Reading	Date	Page

5 Thanks

Title

Psalm 55:22

Page	Date	Bible Reading

5 Thanks

Title

_____

_____

_____

_____

_____

_____

_____

_____

_____

_____

_____

_____

_____

_____

_____

_____

Psalm 55:22

Bible Reading	Date	Page

5 Thanks

Title

_____

_____

_____

_____

_____

_____

_____

_____

_____

_____

_____

_____

_____

_____

_____

_____

Psalm 55:22

Page	Date	Bible Reading

5 Thanks

Title

Psalm 55:22

Bible Reading

Date

Page

5 Thanks

Title

_____

_____

_____

_____

_____

_____

_____

_____

_____

_____

_____

_____

_____

_____

_____

_____

Psalm 55:22

Page	Date	Bible Reading

5 Thanks

Title

_____
_____
_____
_____
_____
_____
_____
_____
_____
_____
_____
_____
_____
_____

Psalm 55:22

Bible Reading	Date	Page

5 Thanks

Title

_____

_____

_____

_____

_____

_____

_____

_____

_____

_____

_____

_____

_____

_____

_____

_____

_____

Psalm 55:22

Page	Date	Bible Reading

5 Thanks

Title

Psalm 55:22

Bible Reading

Date

Page

5 Thanks

Title

Psalm 55:22

Page	Date	Bible Reading

5 Thanks

Title

_____

_____

_____

_____

_____

_____

_____

_____

_____

_____

_____

_____

_____

_____

_____

_____

Psalm 55:22

Bible Reading

Date

Page

5 Thanks

Title

_____

_____

_____

_____

_____

_____

_____

_____

_____

_____

_____

_____

_____

_____

_____

_____

_____

_____

Psalm 55:22

Page	Date	Bible Reading

5 Thanks

Title

Psalm 55:22

Bible Reading	Date	Page

5 Thanks

Title

_____

_____

_____

_____

_____

_____

_____

_____

_____

_____

_____

_____

_____

_____

_____

_____

_____

Psalm 55:22

Page	Date	Bible Reading

5 Thanks

Title

_____

_____

_____

_____

_____

_____

_____

_____

_____

_____

_____

_____

_____

_____

_____

Psalm 55:22

Bible Reading	Date	Page

5 Thanks

Title

Psalm 55:22

Page	Date	Bible Reading

5 Thanks

Title

_____

_____

_____

_____

_____

_____

_____

_____

_____

_____

_____

_____

_____

_____

_____

Psalm 55:22

Bible Reading	Date	Page

5 Thanks

Title

Psalm 55:22

Page	Date	Bible Reading

5 Thanks

Title

_____

_____

_____

_____

_____

_____

_____

_____

_____

_____

_____

_____

_____

_____

Psalm 55:22

Bible Reading	Date	Page

5 Thanks

Title

_____
_____
_____
_____
_____
_____
_____
_____
_____
_____
_____
_____
_____
_____
_____
_____
_____

Psalm 55:22

Page	Date	Bible Reading

5 Thanks

Title

Psalm 55:22

Bible Reading	Date	Page

5 Thanks

Title

_____

_____

_____

_____

_____

_____

_____

_____

_____

_____

_____

_____

_____

_____

_____

_____

Psalm 55:22

Page	Date	Bible Reading

5 Thanks

Title

Psalm 55:22

Bible Reading	Date	Page

5 Thanks

Title

_____

_____

_____

_____

_____

_____

_____

_____

_____

_____

_____

_____

_____

_____

_____

_____

Psalm 55:22

Page	Date	Bible Reading

5 Thanks

Title

_____

_____

_____

_____

_____

_____

_____

_____

_____

_____

_____

_____

_____

_____

_____

_____

_____

_____

_____

_____

Psalm 55:22

Bible Reading	Date	Page

5 Thanks

Title

Psalm 55:22

Page	Date	Bible Reading

5 Thanks

Title

Psalm 55:22

Bible Reading	Date	Page

5 Thanks

Title

Psalm 55:22

A Lake Surfer's Journey
by Jack Nordgren

Paperback: 108 pages
Product Dimensions: 8.1 x 5.3 x 0.4 inches

"A Lake Surfer's Journey" is available online.

This is story about a lake surfer who comes to the end of himself and becomes a believer in Jesus Christ. He not only gives his life to God but also his surfboard. God gives his surfboard back to him and takes him and his family to Hawaii for almost 30 years to plant a church in Waikiki Beach. Then brings him and his wife back to the Midwest to plant a church on WEKO beach and surf on lake Michigan. Read Chapter One: **http://southshorefellowship.org/lakesurfer**

For more about the author, news on upcoming projects and discussions, please go to: **http://bit.ly/jack-nordgren**

Made in the USA
Charleston, SC
07 September 2012